Ice Cream, Hot Chocolate, and More

For my children, Jackson and Kayla Grace, who make me smile each day.

Ice Cream, Hot Chocolate, and More

Written and Illustrated by
Kourtney H. Grant

Text copyright © 2017 by Kourtney Grant

Cover design © 2017 by Kourtney Grant

Illustrations © 2017 by Kourtney Grant

All rights reserved. No part of this book may be reproduced or transmitted in any form or by any means, electronic or mechanical, including photocopying, recording, or by an information storage and retrieval system, without written permission from the publisher.

ISBN-13: 978-0692937983

JK Publishing
P.O. Box 323
Rockville, VA 23146

Printed in the United States

I love you more than

three scoops of your favorite *ice cream*.

I love you more than

a sloppy, wet kiss from ***your pup***.

I love you more than

Movie Night on the big, blue couch.

I love you more than

slow sips of *hot chocolate* by a crackling fire.

I love you more than

a quick, whoosh down *the slide*.

I love you more than

soothing ***songs*** of angels in the wooden rocking chair.

I love you more than

chunky *chicken nuggets* smothered in ketchup.

I love you more than

a bouncy *piggy back ride* through the house.

I love you more than

a gazillion *gifts* for your birthday.

I love you more

and more

each day!

A flood of gratitude flows from my heart. Thanks to my parents, Joseph and Kathleen, for instilling within me a love for family and devotion to God.

Special thanks go to my husband, Jay, for supporting me along the way. Thanks to my children, Jackson and Kayla Grace, for inspiring me with your genuine laughter and love.

To my siblings, Kristin and Coleman, thank you for your encouraging words.

Fellow author, Ms. Elaine Hopkins, your guidance was invaluable.

God gave me vision and strength. I'm grateful for the experiences He allowed that were stepping stones to creating and completing this project. Thank you.

www.ingramcontent.com/pod-product-compliance
Lightning Source LLC
Chambersburg PA
CBHW041745040426
42444CB00001B/32